A GENTLEMAN'S GUIDE TO ETIQUETTE

CLINTON T. GREENLEAF III

Adams Media Corporation
Avon, Massachusetts

Published by
Adams Media Corporation
57 Littlefield Street, Avon, MA 02322, USA
www.adamsmedia.com

ISBN: 1-58062-560-6

Printed in Canada.

J I H G F E D C B A

Library of Congress Cataloging-in-Publication
Greenleaf, Clinton T.
A gentleman's guide to etiquette / by Clinton T. Greenleaf, III.
p.   cm.
Includes bibliographical references.
ISBN 1-58062-560-6
1. Etiquette for men. I. Title

BJ1985 .G74   2001
395.1'42--dc21   2001046347

This publication is designed to provide accurate and authoritative information with regard to the subject matter covered. It is sold with the understanding that the publisher is not engaged in rendering legal, accounting,
or other professional advice. If legal advice or other expert assistance is
required, the services of a competent professional person should be sought.
—From a *Declaration of Principles* jointly adopted by a Committee
of the American Bar Association and a Committee of
Publishers and Associations.

Cover photo by Superstock.

*This book is available at quantity discounts for bulk purchases.
For information, call 1-800-872-5627.*

DISCLAIMER

This guide was written to offer options to the professional male. It should not be considered a guide to a strict code of conduct. Following the advice in this book does not guarantee any specific benefits.

DEDICATION

This book is dedicated to my family: my parents, Helen and Geof, and my sister, Julie (aka Sister Nikareti). Thank you for your love, guidance, and support. I love you.

CONTENTS

PREFACE

From the first grade through high school, I attended a wonderful school named University School. It is right outside Cleveland, Ohio, and I have some great memories of my time there. I can clearly remember that on my first day in 1980, we were instructed to learn and understand the school motto: Responsibility, Loyalty, and Consideration.

At the time I had no idea of the magnitude of these three seemingly simple words, but over the twelve years I spent at University and the years at Holy Cross in the Marine ROTC Program, I learned how important they were. My experiences proved, time and time again, that these three words were the keys to proper conduct. When I put my appreciation of these words to work in the business world, I was considered a "business etiquette expert" by the *Wall Street Journal*. Etiquette might not be the only reason you are hired, but you will see in this book that it will help you get a job and develop your career.

This book, and its companion, *A Gentleman's Guide to Appearance*, began as a collection of notes that I wrote to help a few of my friends in college get an edge on job interviews. The idea was to help young men who were smart and talented but needed some guidance with the basics of acting like gentlemen. Through no fault of their own, they had not been taught these rules and tricks of the trade. At a time when many young men do not know the basics of professional appearance and conduct, those who are knowledgeable have a clear advantage. The great news is that anyone can learn how to act properly, and this book will teach you the fundamentals.

The essence of etiquette is how to act properly in different situations. I look at it in a simple way. Etiquette is a healthy mix of professionalism and personality. The best rules are the ones that build your credibility with your coworkers and clients and allow you to focus on your business.

INTRODUCTION

Let's face it—in today's world appearance and conduct matter. People are initially judged by the way they look. They earn their credibility based on how they act. Those who want to succeed take the time to look their best and act appropriately on all occasions.

By reading this book, you can learn to look great and conduct yourself like a professional. You will learn that attention to detail matters, not only in your career but in all aspects of your life. The level of care reflected in your appearance and manners attracts positive attention and admiration, which fosters confidence. Most important, you will begin to pay more attention to detail, a skill that is highly valued in the professional world.

We will build an understanding of the foundations of etiquette through the use of basic building blocks. Each block depends on those that precede it, so be sure to read the book in order. As you study each block, you will build integral parts of your etiquette; once you understand all the segments, you will quickly master the basics of etiquette.

PART I
APPEARANCE

CLOTHING 1

A large part of etiquette is looking the part. You cannot be taken seriously if you do not wear appropriate clothing. This is the first building block because, like it or not, it is the first item people use when developing an impression. Although we will not delve deeply into what is considered professional dress, we should spend some time on the basics.

You need to know "when to turn it on and when to turn it off." This is the case with your sense of humor, attitude, and clothing. There are times to be funny or dress with flair, and times to be conservative, especially with your wardrobe. Knowing what to wear and when is integral.

PROFESSIONAL DRESS

In the professional world, a suit is normal dress. The casual workplace has changed this tradition somewhat, but the general rule is still in place: When you are in a professional setting, wearing a tailored suit is a good start. No matter how polished your etiquette may be, if you look underdressed, others will not take you seriously.

Your wardrobe, then, should consist of well-tailored jackets and pants, matching ties, dress shirts, and a few pairs of well shined shoes. Even though you may have a number of fun suits and ties, you should try to maintain a conservative look with standard-color suits of navy and charcoal and a professional looking tie. The office is usually not the place to show your modern sense of style or collection of funny ties.

Formal Wear

A black-tie event is still common in business and must be taken seriously. Men have it pretty easy at black-tie parties. A tux, a cummerbund and bow tie, a white pleated shirt, and patent leather shoes are the norm. If you've stopped growing, consider buying a tuxedo to avoid the hassles of renting one. The only real choice you have with your tux is the color of your bow tie and cummerbund. Black is considered standard and safe, but you may choose to purchase a few extra colors or patterns for your wardrobe.

A white-tie event is more formal and requires a longer jacket (also called tails), a white bow tie, and a white vest. The rest of the wardrobe is the same as for a black-tie occasion. You may see on some invitations the phrase "Black tie optional." This used to mean that you had the option of wearing tails or a standard tuxedo. Now it usually means (and is often interpreted to mean) that you may wear a tuxedo or a suit. To stay safe and look fine, wear a tuxedo and you'll be in great company.

BUSINESS CASUAL

Business casual is the new trend in professional circles, but what that means is still somewhat in question. As a general guide, if you are at all unsure about how casual you can be, don't guess. Wear appropriate professional clothing on the first casual day and observe what your coworkers wear. Depending on your type of business, the weather, your city, and the standards of casual dressing in your office, what is considered casual may vary greatly.

Khakis or dark dress pants are generally acceptable everywhere. With a collared, button-down shirt, you can fit into almost any casual workplace. When weather permits, a golf or polo shirt may be acceptable; however, jeans often are not, so check with your coworkers before you risk it. Hats are never appropriate, nor are T-shirts or shorts. You can wear casual shoes, boat shoes, loafers, or even your usual dress shoes if they match the rest of your outfit. In the winter, a sweater is a good idea. Be sure to wear a collared shirt underneath the sweater, though. Finally, remember that you do have coworkers, so don't forget your socks.

Clothing Accessories

Now that your clothes are set, you need accessories. For starters, you need a business watch. This is a watch that looks professional with your suits but is not too flashy. As a general rule, leather and metal bands (gold, silver, and stainless steel) are advisable. Avoid digital faces and plastic bands.

Another important accessory is a leather belt. You will need one black belt and one brown belt, or a single convertible belt, with a nice silver or gold buckle. Remember, though, you are not a cowboy, so keep the buckle small.

Many professionals look great wearing braces, also called suspenders. Suspenders are a substitute for a belt, so wear one or the other but not both. The key to wearing suspenders properly is to pay to have buttons sewn onto your pants to anchor the straps. No self-respecting professional wears clip-on suspenders. The color of your suspenders should match your tie. As usual, choosing a solid color or basic pattern makes matching much easier. Also remember that outlandish colors may not be appropriate.

OFFICE ACCESSORIES

Buy a high-quality pen. Avoid carrying a cheap pen during any interview or meeting. You can find a nice pen for about $10, but don't be afraid to pay a bit more for quality. A prestigious pen will really make you look good, just as a cheap pen can detract from your professional appearance. Mont Blanc, Waterman, and Cross are premier manufacturers of high-quality pens.

Along with the pen, it is advisable to carry a leather-bound portfolio for important documents and your business cards. You can buy a generic portfolio or carry one from your school or company. The idea is to carry loose papers in a professional looking way at all times. If you need to carry several items, a leather or metal briefcase can be a fine accessory. Make sure, however, that the briefcase looks professional and not like an old gym bag. It is also important to keep your briefcase neat and organized. If a client or coworker sees your messy briefcase, he or she may rightly assume that you are sloppy and irresponsible.

PERSONAL ACCESSORIES

Use cologne sparingly; people are usually turned off by an overpowering scent. As a general rule, about half the amount you would use if you were going on a date is proper for the office. Put it on about fifteen minutes before you leave your house because it takes a few minutes to dissipate. Use cologne to enhance your appearance, not dominate it.

Clean hands are imperative in business. A manicure might not be necessary (although many businessmen do get weekly manicures), but it is important to keep your hands and fingernails clean. Your fingernails should be trimmed (not bitten) cleanly just past the quick. This will give you about a sixteenth of an inch of white at the end of each nail.

PHYSICAL FITNESS 3

A discussion of professionalism would be incomplete without at least mentioning the benefits of staying, or getting, in shape. Although there are successful professionals who succeed without being fit, most truly successful businessmen are in great shape. They spend the time to work out and tone their bodies. They also have more stamina and are able to deal more easily with working under pressure and consistent late hours. Make the time to work out: You will have more energy, and you will look like a mover and shaker.

Your professional career is predicated on your ability to deal with things like stress, pressure, long hours, and the occasional sprint through the airport to catch a flight. A good routine that includes stretching, a cardiovascular workout (running or swimming), and strength training will help you increase your stamina for those long nights at the office. When you finally get home, being in shape will help you fall asleep faster and sleep more soundly.

Pressure at the office will seem much less overwhelming if you can keep fit; somehow an overdue report isn't as daunting if you just made it through a 4-mile hill run that morning. And then there is always the increased confidence that comes from looking your best.

People often do business with people who are confident and enthusiastic. Why not use this to your advantage?

This does not mean that your career depends on four hours a day in the gym. By taking about one hour every other day, you can trim down, keep your heart in shape, and have more energy. After consulting with your doctor, establish a regular workout plan. Decide the time of day you will work out and what you will do. Allow about an hour for your workout, plus time to cool down and shower afterward. If you do this every other day for a month, you will see a positive change in your appearance.

PART II
PERSONAL
INTERACTION

PERSONAL BASICS   4

Etiquette is also displayed in the way you treat and interact with people, from the CEO to the most junior assistant. Thus, the second building block in your etiquette development is the basics of personal interaction. You can use my school motto—Responsibility, Loyalty, and Consideration—to guide you in your personal interactions.

RESPONSIBILITY

It seems that in today's culture, responsibility is an antiquated notion. Many people are unwilling to take responsibility for negative situations and instead prefer to call themselves victims. This "victim-it is" is common in professional circles as well. Fight this disease with all your might; when you are given a task, take responsibility for your actions. If you succeed, that's wonderful; give credit to everyone who helped you. If you do not, learn from it, and take full responsibility for the error. Although this might seem to be a game plan that will get you fired quickly, it will, in fact, do the opposite. Your boss, coworkers, and subordinates will respect you as one of the few people in the professional arena who takes responsibility for his actions. It is also the right thing to do, and doing what is right is a fundamental part of etiquette.

Loyalty

Loyalty is another trait that is often dismissed in our culture. Loyalty to your company, your boss, your coworkers, and your subordinates is integral in building strong interpersonal relationships. To be clear, I am not recommending blind loyalty; when you are trusted with information at task, fulfill your duty and you will reap the rewards. Disloyalty, on the other hand, will ruin your reputation. Then, no matter how sharply you dress or how good your table manners are, you will never be respected.

Remember that after Benedict Arnold defected to the British during the Revolutionary War, the English commanders never trusted him with a battle command because of his earlier disloyalty. If you are disloyal, no one—not even those you help—will be able to trust you.

Consideration

Consideration in the form of empathy, not sympathy, is a large part of etiquette. Being considerate of others illustrates your attempt to understand situations before you make snap judgments. Given the option, people will almost always work with someone who is open and thoughtful rather than rash and impulsive. These three traits—responsibility, loyalty, and consideration—will help guide you in your relationships and build the basics of etiquette in your life.

HUMOR

While business is often serious, there is no harm in having a healthful sense of humor. Some companies are known for the fun they have, and they reap healthful benefits as a direct result of that fun. There are many different kinds of humor, from a dry wit to a more biting style. Although some biting comments may be funny or even accurate, be sure you are not laughing or making jokes at another's expense. There is no exception to this rule, even if the person you are insulting is not going to find out about your joke.

So, how can you show humor in the workplace? Self-effacing humor is a fantastic way to make good jokes while showing that you are confident and able to poke fun at yourself. Another added benefit of this type of humor is that if you make a mistake and make light of your folly, it is much more difficult for others to hold you in contempt for the error. Your confidence will impress them. By making the joke, you are effectively admitting that you messed up and that it is not the end of the world.

5 THE PLATINUM RULE

Every company, group, or family has at least one person who is friendly with everyone. You know the type; he or she is always smiling, is nice to everyone, and seems to be everyone's friend. These people are the way they are because they make others feel comfortable. No matter the minor differences of wealth, class, intelligence, or background, all people are worthy of respect and these people realize it.

What do they know that others do not? They are masters of the "platinum rule." The Golden Rule, made famous in kindergarten, states that one should treat others as one would like to be treated. This rule is a good start, but people often have different expectations of how they want to be treated. Recognizing this truth, the platinum rule says that one should treat others *the way they want to be treated*. Those who are skilled in etiquette realize this caveat and pay attention to others.

Most people are not cryptic. They let you know what they like and how they want to be treated. While some people are very serious in the workplace, others laugh all day long. Assuming either demeanor does not affect performance, both personality types are acceptable and prevalent. By following the platinum rule, you can be serious with those who prefer to be serious and more jovial with those who are more relaxed. Your job, as someone who works to embody etiquette, is to pay attention and treat people the way they want to be treated.

The platinum rule allows you to make others feel comfortable in your presence and treat you well. Although etiquette is based primarily on a set of rules, your ability to follow those rules is useless if you cannot interact properly with people.

6 YOUR SUPPORT STAFF

It is a mistake to think that you can get away with ignoring or treating support staff poorly. Proper etiquette requires you to treat everyone with respect and dignity. Breech this code and you will suffer. Professionals know that their successes are based on the quality of their staff and they rely on them heavily. A good manager is aware of who treats his or her people properly and who does not. Many managers will take it personally if their staff is poorly treated; it will be as if you had been rude to them directly.

You will find that asking people for favors is a much more fruitful endeavor if you have always treated them with dignity. If you need an assistant to work late, or someone in the mailroom to rush an overnight package to the airport, keep in mind that the staff will remember how you have treated them (and their colleagues) in the past. This sort of word, good or bad, spreads quickly. The entire office will know how you treat others. Don't expect to get away with treating the boss well and the staff poorly. You will be exposed quickly and then neither group will trust you.

When a member of your staff successfully completes a task, take the time to praise the individual in public for his or her effort. One of the best management traits you can develop is to effectively praise subordinates for a job well done. You don't have to throw a party in the person's honor for every achievement, sometimes a simple memo or a genuine thank you will do. But taking the time to recognize the work in front of his or her peers will foster support for you and will keep the staff loyal and motivated.

Unfortunately, people make mistakes from time to time. Before you rush to place the blame for the incident, make sure of two things. First, make sure the problem is solved. If the computer system fails, fix it before you yell at the staff. Second, make sure you have your facts straight. All too often, in an attempt to vent his or her frustration, a boss will yell at an innocent employee. That behavior only succeeds in making a fool out of the boss.

After you have determined what happened and why, then dispense your judgment. As important as it is for you to remember to praise in public, you must remember to reprimand in private. Making a spectacle of someone's error will destroy your credibility and leadership presence.

A client's staff can be a huge help to you as well. If you have a good relationship with a client's secretary, you can count on extra help when you need it. This also goes for prospects; that is, those with whom you want to do business in the future. If you call on someone who is interested in doing business with your company, he or she will almost always ask the receptionist how you behaved while you were waiting and how you spoke and acted. It would be a great help to have an extra cheerleader in your camp, so remember to respect everyone.

Never underestimate the number of times you will have to call a client, needing to speak about an important issue, and be at the mercy of his or her staff. If you have a good relationship with the staff, many more doors will open and more opportunities will become available.

This is an important rule to keep in mind when interviewing at prospective employers as well. A "greeter" will often take your coat and make you as comfortable as possible. This person will also answer any questions you have before the process starts. The greeter is usually younger than you and will act like a friend, but never doubt that everything you say and do will be reported back to the person making the hiring decision. Treat the greeter with respect and you will benefit immensely; act irresponsibly and you will suffer.

PART III
COMMUNICATION

NONVERBAL COMMUNICATION 8

In the business world, those who do not follow the rules of accepted behavior lose; it is as simple as that. One major aspect of etiquette is demeanor, or what you say and how you act in a professional setting. In its simplest form, demeanor can include things like posture and attitude. There is no question that a positive attitude is a helpful aspect of etiquette and a basic building block as well. People react more favorably to individuals who have good posture and who smile. Notice that a calm smile is called for here, not a wide, goofy grin. A calm smile exudes dignity and power and is proven to relax others around you.

POSTURE

Posture is often ignored, but you convey a great deal of nonverbal communication with your posture. Others interpret the way you sit, stand, and walk as keys to your attitude, strength, and ability to accomplish difficult tasks. Go-getters sit up straight, stand with style, and walk tall. People who are in a rut often sulk and sink down. So, how should you carry yourself?

Sitting

Sit as if you have a string attached to your chest and shoulders. Imagine that the string is pulling you up, so that you sit up straight. This will allow you to think more clearly, feel more energetic, and look professional.

Standing

When standing, fight the urge to put your hands in your pockets, fold your arms, or move your hands. If you are constantly fidgeting, you will attract attention to your body and away from your words. When waiting or speaking with someone, the most professional way to stand is with your hands at your sides in a relaxed position. This conveys a willingness to listen, patience, and professionalism. If you must do something with your hands, clasp them behind your back in a somewhat relaxed manner.

You take away from your credibility when you walk hunched over. As you are walking, imagine that the string that was attached to your chest and shoulders is now moving with you, keeping your shoulders and head straight and your chin up. Smile when you walk. Grim-acing makes you appear angry; smiling helps boost your attitude.

Face-to-Face Communication 9

Many rules of etiquette are pretty obvious and may already be part of your personality. For example, you should avoid emotional topics of conversation (such as religion and politics) and use Standard English (no slang, jargon, or vernacular).

When speaking to others, look them in the eye; this also goes for listening. When you look at a person with a desire to listen, you show that the individual is important to you and is worthy of your time. If you are tired or bored, fight the urge to yawn or glance away with an annoyed look on your face.

It is also a good idea to take along a pen and paper when you go to a meeting or travel in your car. You never know when someone will tell you something important that you need to remember. Even if your memory is great, write it down. Having a paper trail is helpful in business; it saves the embarrassment of having to ask a question twice.

10 TELEPHONE ETIQUETTE

Because so much business is conducted over the telephone, it is important to develop good phone skills. Make sure to speak clearly and at a moderate pace. You do not want your clients to have to constantly ask you to repeat what you just said because you mumbled or spoke too quickly. Smile when you speak and be cordial. Although it sounds crazy, people can hear the smile in your voice when you are on the telephone. Since many professionals today never meet their clients face to face, the telephone is their only link. For these people, a professional phone voice and demeanor are incredibly important. To be sure you are making the proper impression, ask your family, friends, and coworkers to listen to how you sound on the phone. If you think you need help, consider hiring a voice coach. A voice coach is not very expensive, and he or she can really help you improve your telephone and speaking skills.

PERSONAL CALLS

While at the office, you may need to make a few personal calls over the course of the day. Although most employers are willing to allow personal calls, be sure to keep them to a minimum because they detract from your productivity. If your boss constantly hears you making personal calls, it will hurt your career. If subordinates hear you making personal calls, it will weaken your credibility as well as encourage them to do the same.

The speakerphone is a fantastic invention that has helped people accomplish other tasks while on the phone. Unfortunately, it is not appropriate for most business calls. If you receive permission, then use the speakerphone; more often than not, its use is considered rude. The other party does not know if your coworkers are listening to the conversation, what else is going on, or why he or she is not important enough to get your complete attention. So, unless you are sitting on hold, use the receiver or a headset.

Voice Mail

Voice mail is growing in popularity. Most offices use it as a basic communications tool. Although voice mail is, in many ways, an informal means of communication, remember that you are a professional and need to conduct yourself as one when you use it. In a voice mail, greet the person, convey your point clearly, and, above all, keep the message short. Most voice-mail systems allow you to erase and rerecord your messages if you make a mistake. Take advantage of this option; you always want to sound your best. This may mean taking extra time to learn how to use the system, but it is time well spent.

The same goes for your outgoing message. Before recording it, listen to a few of your coworkers and find a good style with which you feel comfortable. If you can easily change the message, consider recording a daily message announcing your availability. If this is too time consuming, select a standard greeting that will prompt the caller for a complete message. No matter how often you change the message be sure it conveys enough information to be helpful to the caller.

Try something like "Hello. You have reached (first and last name). I'm sorry I cannot take your call now, but if you would please leave your name and telephone number, I will return your call as soon as possible."

LANGUAGE

The language you use in the professional world is important. An extensive vocabulary can quickly illustrate your intelligence and creativity. At the same time, there is no excuse for swearing in the office. It might seem cool or part of being a big shot, but no gentleman swears in the workplace. The extensive use of four-letter words shows an inability to learn the English language and usually is characteristic of someone who is inconsiderate to his coworkers and clients. If you must express your disdain, show intelligence and creativity by using more descriptive words.

Learn a valuable lesson from the cartoons and movies geared toward children. Listen to the ways villains express their anger and pick your favorite. Some of the better ones are "rats," "blast," and, "gadzooks!" It is your responsibility to contain your anger and limit your use of expletives.

If you change this element of your conduct and use silly terms, you will accomplish two valuable objectives. First, you will show your colleagues and clients that you respect them enough not to swear in front of them. Second, you stand a pretty good chance of getting them to laugh and see your humorous side when you shout "Blast!" Working to stop swearing and better express yourself in the professional setting will enhance your image among your coworkers and clients.

During the course of a long business day, there are many tasks that just don't get done. This happens to everyone and is understandable. However, there are some things that you must do. Returning phone calls—even those you do not want to make—is one of the tasks you must do every day. As one of the few professionals who returns phone calls, you will set yourself above the many businesspeople who think (incorrectly) that they are too busy to return calls.

11 CELL PHONE ETIQUETTE

In the past few years, the incredible proliferation of new mobile phone options has left us with many questions of etiquette. We've all seen rude people babbling on their cell phones in public places, from restaurants to all forms of public transportation to movie theaters. This new technology infiltrated society faster than we could establish some basic rules for its use. What follows is a general guide that anyone can follow to be more civilized and considerate when using mobile phones.

The first basic rule is that when you are in a public place or in the company of people you consider important, turn the ringer on your phone off. Since cell phones now have voice-mail, you'll be well served by eliminating these interruptions. If you absolutely must take a call, set the phone on silent or vibrate and politely excuse yourself to answer the call.

If you find yourself needing to talk in a public place, keep the conversation short and quiet. With the new digital phones, you can speak softly and still be heard. Remember how annoying it is to listen to a long one-sided telephone conversation, so keep it short. Ask the other person for a better time to talk and end the call.

If you find yourself driving and talking on the phone, realize that it might be smarter, and safer, to pull over to finish the call. You might also consider purchasing a hands-free unit for your phone. Statistics show that talking on a cell phone while driving is just as dangerous as driving while intoxicated. Some cities have passed laws against driving while talking on a cell phone, so play it safe and pull over or get a headset.

As recently as five years ago, cell phones were only for the business elite and for emergencies. Now that so many people are using them in so many different places, it is imperative that we all follow general etiquette rules. Treat the people around you as though they are more important than anything else occurring at that moment, including your phone, and your etiquette will be evident.

12 WRITTEN COMMUNICATION

Many first impressions are made through written communication. The way you communicate through the written word gives others an idea of your intelligence, schooling, and business acumen. Although the assumptions may not be accurate, they quickly become part of the impression you create. Becoming a great writer takes years of hard work, but there are some elements that everyone should follow. Whether you are a wordsmith painting a written picture or simply writing to convey information on paper, using standard communication guidelines is essential to good etiquette.

The most famous and most popular book on proper style is *The Elements of Style*, also known simply by the names of the authors, Strunk and White. This book contains a complete discussion of proper communication from business to personal correspondence. It is a great reference tool and a must for the professional.

Regardless of what form of communication you choose, be sure to proofread the item before you send it out. Although your computer's spell checker will pick up some of the items, it may not get those words that are spelled correctly but used incorrectly—or a grammatical mistake. If the document is very important, you should have another person review it for errors. Often, when you get close to a document, you will gloss over mistakes because you know what you want to say. Another person will help catch these mistakes.

It is also advisable to use a very readable font in your correspondence. Many computers now come with hundreds of fancy and ornate fonts. Although artistic, some of the more complicated choices are less desirable than a basic, readable font. Layout can vary with each form, but there are basic guidelines that should be followed, especially in your first few years in business.

THE BUSINESS LETTER

A business letter is an important part of professional correspondence. By following the proper format, you will illustrate your knowledge of business culture and you will get your message across effectively. It is best to align all type on the left. Begin your letter with the date, followed by the name and address of the individual to whom you are writing. Next, greet the reader by the name you commonly use in conversation. If you have not met, do not use the person's first name. Make the letter as clear, straightforward, and easy to read as possible. In the first or second sentence, convey the purpose of writing, and then spend the rest of the letter discussing the point.

Do your best to keep the letter to one page; 95 percent of your communications should be limited to one page. Single-space the type but include an extra space between paragraphs. You may or may not indent the first line of each paragraph; that is a matter of personal style.

When you complete the body of the text, conclude with "Sincerely" or "Best regards." Leave a few spaces for your signature and then type your full name.

December 6, 2001

Jane Smith
ABC Company
[Address]
[City, State ZIP]

Dear Ms. Smith:

Thank you for your interest in XYZ Company and our products. As you might know, we are specialists in [specialization] and we can really help your company [achievement].

It would be great to sit down and talk with you as you suggested, [time and date] in your office. I have made careful notes of your areas of interest and will bring the pertinent information to our meeting.

If you have any questions before the meeting, please feel free to call me. Otherwise, I'll look forward to seeing you on [date]. Thanks again for your interest in XYZ Company.

Sincerely,

John Q. Doe

John Q. Doe
[Title]

THE BUSINESS MEMO

The proper format for a business memo is constantly changing, but the following is a basic template. First, type "Memorandum" in capital letters to signify the format.

Next, justify all type on the left, and begin with the date. Then skip three lines, and identify the recipient by his or her complete name preceded by "To:". Next, type "From:" and your full name. Below the names, type "Re:" or "Subj:" and then indicate the reason for your communication. This should be a three- or four-word phrase describing the memo. Then write your paragraphs as separate groups, without indenting the first line. No conclusion is necessary. Again, keep your memo to one page. After you have printed it out, initial it to the right of your name.

MEMORANDUM

DATE: October 23, 2001
TO: All Employees   *JQD*
FROM: John Q. Doe, HR Director
RE: Halloween Party

After several months of meetings and employee surveys, the human resources department has decided to host our annual Halloween Party in the office on Halloween afternoon.

The entire day of Halloween will be a casual day for those of you who wish to dress up in a festive costume. Refreshments will be provided, but we ask that you each bring a bag of candy for needy children.

Any questions may be forwarded to me via voice-mail at x1040 or e-mail.

In your correspondence, it is important to encourage the recipients to contact you. Even though the information is included in the letterhead, add a direct phone number or e-mail address for immediate contact. This makes you appear more accessible and will make it easier for others to communicate with you.

13 E-MAIL COMMUNICATION

E-mail is now a common form of communication in most workplaces. Many employees connect to the Internet and communicate with friends and family all over the world on company time. Some employers condone this; others do not. Be sure to check your company's policy on personal e-mail during working hours before unnecessarily endangering your job.

With e-mail, you can often include what is called a "signature." This is a two- to five-line tag that follows any message you send. It should include your name and phone number at a minimum but it can also include your title, company, Web site, or other pertinent information. Begin your e-mail with the proper salutation, use professional language, and keep it short.

Problems can arise when employees believe that the e-mail messages they send are private. By law, your employer can read all e-mail that you send and receive at work. It is unclear how many companies check messages, but the important point is that the possibility exists. When using e-mail at work, assume that your boss and everyone else will read every word you write.

If you feel the need to send personal e-mail, establish a personal account through an Internet Service Provider. There are also several free e-mail services on the

Internet. Realize, though, that the same laws exist for surfing the Internet and visiting the Web. Your employer can track the time you spend and the locations you visit on the Web when using your company's system, so be careful. If you do visit sites that you would not want the entire office to know about, surf the Net away from work. Also, be sparing in your nonbusiness use of the Internet; overuse or misuse could definitely be a career-limiting move.

PART IV
APPLYING
FOR A JOB

WRITING A RESUME AND COVER LETTER

A good resume can help you land the job of your dreams. A bad resume can ensure that you will not get that job. Although many people focus all of their attention on the resume, more time should be spent on the cover letter. What follows are some basic tips that can help you promote yourself through your resume and a brief discussion of the cover letter.

First, and most important, be honest. Aside from the obvious moral problems involved with lying, there are numerous other reasons to tell the truth. For those of you who might be tempted to embellish your resume, pay attention and you will quickly see why you should not.

Interviewers and human resources (HR) professionals are, by their nature, detectives. Most examine every detail with a suspicious eye and are trained to look for lies. Let's be clear: If you lie on your resume and get caught (and that will eventually happen), you will not get the job, or worse, you will be fired after the truth is discovered. Not to mention that people will talk. When the word gets out that you are dishonest, you will lose your coworkers' respect and your career will be over. It is as simple as that.

At the same time, it is important not to be modest. Your resume is the best, and perhaps the only, chance to "toot your own horn." Tell prospective employers about the good things that you have done. If you have accomplished something special, be sure to talk about it. You might think that unless you were the valedictorian, the captain of the football team, and a National Merit Scholar, you have nothing to say, but that is rarely true. Simply look back on the past few years and find things that you have accomplished that will make you more marketable.

John Q. Doe

Home address	School address
Anytown, USA	Collegetown, USA
Home phone	School phone
Home e-mail	School e-mail

OBJECTIVE: To obtain employment at a major public accounting firm.

EDUCATION: **State University,** Class of 2002 Collegetown, USA
Accounting and Finance Major, GPA of 3.4 1998–2002
Honors Society, Dean's List Spring 1999

Central High School, Class of 1998 Anytown, USA
Honors in math, science,and history 1994–1998
Lettered in football and baseball

EMPLOYMENT: **Dewey, Cheatam, and Howe, CPA** Anytown, USA
Summer intern in Audit Department Summer 2000
Learned MS Office and Quickbooks Software

Acme Products, Sales Division Anytown, USA
Sold household products door to door Summer 1999

Tasty Freeze Ice Cream Anytown, USA
Store manager Summer 1998

HOBBIES: **Umpire for Little League** Anytown, USA
Volunteer umpire for local Little League 1997–Present

Reading for the blind Anytown, USA
Read school books for blind children 1999–Present

ORGANIZING THE RESUME

Set up your resume in the following format. Begin with your full name, centered across the top. Use a font size slightly larger than the rest of the resume. If you have one address, center it below your name, along with your phone number and e-mail address. If you have two addresses—for example, if you are in college and live away from home—list both, justifying each against the side columns. Include telephone numbers and e-mail addresses for both.

In discussing addresses and phone numbers, here is one word of caution: Be careful about using your current employer's address, phone number, or e-mail address. Unless you are certain that your current employer will not mind that you are looking for a new job, use only your home address, phone number, and e-mail address. Also, be sure you have an answering machine or voice mail at home. Bear in mind that your potential employer will hear your message, so be certain that it is professional and short as described in Chapter 10.

Next, insert a line separating your name contact information from the body of the resume.

On the first line of text below the break, state your employment objective clearly and professionally. For example, "To obtain full-time employment with a major public accounting firm." If your actual objective is unclear, or if you do not feel comfortable including one, simply leave it out. Keep in mind that you may change objectives and items on the resume to conform to each job for which you are applying.

If you are right out of school, the education section of your resume should come next. If you have been in the professional world for more than a year, you might place the employment section first. Base your decision on what is the most relevant element of your recent past.

Depending on the last level of education completed, you may include or exclude high school data. (If you have a Ph.D., high school information will probably not be of interest to your employers.) If you are a recent college graduate, you probably want to include your high school name, grade point average, any honors received, any sports played, and activities in which you were involved. If you did well, say so. If you were not a star student, do not say anything. The smart move here is to build up your strengths and avoid your weaknesses. To the far right of this information, include the years you were in school, as well as the location of each institution.

Experience or employment history usually comes next. Here you want to focus on your accomplishments, showing the jobs you have had and how they relate to your objective, a prospective position, or your potential employer's business. Discuss your responsibilities, accomplishments, duties performed, and awards received. Show the reader that you have a variety of talents, can handle responsibility, and have been trusted in the past. Companies are much more willing to hire someone who is already "proven." Even if your experience is at an ice-cream store, you can still show that you were responsible, trustworthy, and managed people effectively.

It is common for applicants to have several different resumes that highlight different experiences and jobs. These resumes are tailored to particular companies and industries.

The final section can include your hobbies, interests, and involvement in outside groups. Remember that it is up to you what you include on your resume. If you feel that the inclusion or exclusion of any item is justified and will help a potential employer make a decision in your favor, go for it—just keep your resume to the point. If you are new to the job world, try to keep it to one page.

WRITING THE COVER LETTER

The cover letter is very important; in many cases, it is more important than the actual resume. Each applicant for the job will submit a resume with his or her skills and qualifications, education, experience, and the like. Not everyone will send a cover letter, and even fewer will spend the time to properly personalize it.

Follow the same format for the cover letter as for the business letter discussed in Chapter 12. Focus on how the company will benefit by hiring you. Tell them what makes you unique; that is, what you can do or bring to the company that no one else can. With a personalized letter that speaks directly to the company, you can allude to your resume; but spend your time in this one-page letter convincing the reader that you are the best candidate for the job. Think of it from the employer's side: They want to hire someone who will help them prosper, financially and otherwise. Find the best way to tell them that you will help them achieve these goals, and you'll be at the top of the list. With a great cover letter and resume, you will be in a very good position to be called in for an interview.

HOW TO PREPARE

When you receive an appointment for an interview with a prospective employer, take the time to learn about the company and the job for which you are applying before the interview takes place. The Internet is a great place to start, but company newsletters, annual reports, and magazine articles can also be helpful.

Try to gain a general understanding of the company, just as if you were going to write a report about it. Find out who the top officers are, and if possible, uncover their personality types. Almost without exception, the leader's personality is indicative of the corporate culture. Also study current events involving the company and its industry. You can be sure that most topics in the news will be fair game for the interviewer's questions. Current events will also give you a good base for questions to ask the interviewer.

Make sure to get a good night's rest before your interview. You want to be fresh and alert. Before you leave for your interview, do a final check to make sure you have everything that you need: a clean, crisp, comfortable suit that is free of lint and spots; at least five copies of your resume; your portfolio and pen; and a positive attitude!

WHAT TO DISCUSS

Arrive a few minutes early. Once the interview starts, you will have a short time to get a feel for the interviewer. Build a rapport by sitting up straight, smiling softly, and looking directly into the person's eyes when you speak. The first few minutes will create the interviewer's basic impression of you and, quite possibly, will affect your chances of being hired. Often the interview will begin with a discussion of your resume or an employment form designed by the company. Reviewing this familiar information will help you relax.

As discussed in the resume section, you must be honest. Lying will only make you uncomfortable. You need to be relaxed to freely discuss your accomplishments. Be modest but positive about your experiences, and be sure to explain how you overcame problems or hurdles in your life. Most interviewers now ask you to describe a situation in which you dealt with difficulty or failure, and what you learned in the process.

If you were previously employed, the interviewer will almost always ask about your former employer. This is not an invitation to complain about how horrible your experience was or how much you hate your old boss, even if it is true. This question is designed to evaluate what kind of relationship you had with your previous employer. Be honest, but do not say that your boss hated you or that you hated him or her. Try to mention the benefits of working at the job and what you learned that will help you in your next position. Stay positive about your experience and your interviewer will be impressed.

Candidates often fear the difficult questions that they may have to answer. In general, if you are faced with a question that you cannot solve, do not guess or make up an answer. It is much easier to say "I don't know, but I will find out and call you with the answer tomorrow." You will appear more intelligent and honest, and you will not have to be afraid of the truth.

Concerns and Obstacles

You may face some minor obstacles in your interview. The worst is the question that seems off the wall. Your interviewer may call it a "probing" or "character" question—they're supposed to give the interviewer an insight into what kind of person you are. An example is, "If you could be any kind of fruit, what kind would you be?" If you are asked a question like this, do your best to answer it, but don't stress; there is no "right" answer.

Your interviewer may also ask a question that will test your analytical and problem-solving abilities. It could be a system question or a riddle. A system question tests your problem-solving methods. For example, let's say your interviewer asks, "How many gas stations are there in the United States?" He or she is not asking for the exact amount of gas sold. Rather, the interviewer is trying to discover how you arrive at your answer. These questions will test your assumptions and mathematical calculations for logic but not necessarily for numerical accuracy.

Answer this type of question by thinking it through. Count the number of gas stations in your town. Now estimate the population in your town. Divide the population by the population of the United States. Using ratios, divide the number of gas stations by the percentage of your town's population and you will have a rough but good answer.

Another interview technique is the riddle. Here the interviewer asks you a complex riddle that requires you to think "outside of the box." Knowing how to answer these questions can be very helpful, especially if you have seen the question before. There are several good books on riddles that will give you some samples and some tips on solving new problems.

One of the most famous riddles goes as follows: *You have three items in your possession:—a fox, a chicken, and a bag of grain. If two are left alone together, the fox would eat the chicken and the chicken would eat the grain. Your job is to get all three across a river in a small boat. You can only carry one item over at a time on this boat, so how do you do it?*

Answer: First, carry the chicken over to the other side. The fox will not eat the grain—so far so good. Now go back to the original side and get the fox. Bring him to the new side, but be sure to bring the chicken back with you. Now leave the chicken on the first side and bring the grain over to the new side. Return to get the chicken, and you now have all three on the new side safely!

Another idea is to talk to others who have recently interviewed with the company and ask them for pointers. Since each company is different, it helps to have some insight before you get there.

Dining During an Interview

Often in the interview process, you will be invited to lunch either as part of a full day of interviews or just for a "relaxed" setting. Do not be fooled; this setting is no more relaxing than being in an office. It does, however, give the employer a great chance to see you outside of the office, and it serves as a window to the "true you." If the company does a lot of business over lunch, this test is also very practical. You are always under the microscope, even at lunch. Watch how you treat others, especially the staff at the restaurant.

You may think that because the interviewer is going to pick up the check (and he or she will) you can order anything you want. This is not, however, an invitation to order the most expensive item on the menu. Choose a meal with a moderate price that is easy to eat. In other words, avoid finger foods and any pasta dishes that can really make a mess. You want the interviewer to focus on your ability to work well not on the huge bill and the sauce on your shirt.

A test that interviewers for large companies used in the 1970s was called "The Salt Test." They would check to see if the candidate would put salt or pepper on his or her food before tasting it. They surmised that anyone who would salt their food before tasting it was too quick to judge and thus was not executive material. Although this may seem to be an odd test, some interviewers still use it. So, even if you love salt or pepper, make sure you taste your food first. It's pretty easy to do, and it could save you from making a huge mistake.

ASKING QUESTIONS

At the end of every interview, you will be given an opportunity to ask questions. Use it. Find out what you want to know but have not been able to learn from your initial research. Having said that, there is a line that you should not cross when asking questions in an interview situation. This can include asking how much money the position pays, the vacation policy, what the company does, and what your chances are of getting the job. Instead ask something that will help you to be chosen above other candidates. Ask about a "day in the life" of the person currently in the position for which you are applying, or how the company can offer you growth, both personally and professionally. Depending on the interviewer's perceived receptivity for suggestions, you may want to use your earlier research on the company to suggest a new opportunity they might consider. Many companies would appreciate this initiative.

AFTER THE INTERVIEW

After the interview, be sure to follow up with a written thank-you letter to the interviewer or interviewers. This can take the form of a card or letter but not an e-mail. The most important part is to thank the individual for his or her time and consideration. You may also answer any questions you were unable to answer during the interview, provide other information, or ask another question. Be sure to personalize the communication by making a reference to your interview. If you met with more than one person, be sure to send separate thank-you letters to each and mail them in separate envelopes. Be sure to send your thank-you note as soon as you get home, preferably on the same day as the interview.

PART V
THE RULES
OF ETIQUETTE

CHIVALRY: THE BEGINNING 16

Chivalry, still considered a noble concept, is the parent of modern etiquette. Many of the customs that are embodied in proper etiquette were born in the chivalric code of the Middle Ages.

Those who say chivalry is dead are wrong. Those who say chivalry is chauvinistic are also wrong. A true gentleman treats both men and women with respect and is willing to help anyone in need. While there may be a few people who do not appreciate an act of chivalry, no man is ever faulted for treating others with respect and dignity.

So, how does one learn the rules of chivalry? The governing principle is that a busy person can take a few extra seconds out of his day to help make other people's lives easier. Treat others as if they are the most important people in the world, even if you are more interested in other things. Many of the concepts are quite basic and are probably already part of your subconscious thought. If not, you might want to practice them until they become ingrained.

For example, when you get to a door first, hold it open for others before you enter. After you have gone through the door, look to see if you could hold it for someone else. It might take an extra five or six seconds, but you will garner respect and show your etiquette skills in the process.

Elevator etiquette is also born of the chivalric code. When entering an elevator, wait for all the people who are exiting at that floor to leave and hold the door for anyone who might be waiting. Then you may enter the elevator. If there is enough room in the car, stand to the side; do not invade anyone's personal space. If you are traveling with a coworker, do not discuss confidential information; you have no idea who might be listening. It is also rude to force others in the car to listen to your conversation. When you reach your floor, hold the door from the inside for anyone who is leaving and, once you exit, for anyone who wants to get into the elevator.

When guests are visiting your office, offer to take their coats and ask if they would like a drink. If you show them to another room, hold the door and wait for the group to enter before you do. Take care of your guests and they will notice your attention to detail and etiquette. Similarly, when at a restaurant with a client, coworker, or friend, offer to take the other person's coat. Once you finally sit down, offer to push the chair in for any woman who needs assistance. Of course women can do this for themselves, but you are showing, with your offer, that you know how to treat others properly.

When you are walking down the street with a woman, take the position on the outside, closer to the cars. This is considered old-fashioned but extremely classy. This rule started back in the era of packed-dirt streets, horse-drawn carriages, and flowing dresses. When the rain soaked the streets, a thick layer of mud would form. Passing carriages would then splatter the mud onto the pedestrians. In an effort to spare the ladies the expense of cleaning their many-layered dresses, the gentlemen would walk on the outside. The splashing mud from the carriages would then land on them instead of on the ladies.

Although the pragmatic need to stand on the outside is considerably lessened in this modern era of paved streets, most observant people will see the gentlemanly nature of your acts and be impressed that you know how to treat people properly. Women who are aware of this tradition will also be quite impressed. When you get to a car, open the door for others first, and then you may enter. Remember that the most senior person should sit in the most comfortable seat, usually in the front. It is a good rule to be the last one into the car, especially if you are driving. If you have any control over the radio, seriously consider keeping it off. Unless you are certain that everyone enjoys your taste in music, you should try to eliminate the controversy. If others object, allow them to pick the station. When riding in public transportation, offer your seat to a woman or elderly person; they might not accept, but it is a kind and gentlemanly gesture.

A brief discussion of sexual harassment is integral to any etiquette book and this seems to be the perfect place for it. In the past ten years, society has finally begun to recognize the dangers of sexual harassment. As a general rule, avoid questionable behavior and material in the workplace. Your personal life is your own—but as soon as you assume working responsibilities, you are under the microscope. If anyone can perceive your behavior as sexual harassment, you are in trouble. At the office avoid jokes, e-mail, and conversation that can be construed as sexual. You may miss

out on a laugh or two, but the risk of a sexual harassment suit is just not worth it.

The concepts of chivalry and gender equality are not
mutually exclusive. A true gentleman knows that by
being chivalrous he is simply being kind and considerate; he is not asserting his dominance. Follow the
basics of chivalry to see the more detailed elements of
modern business etiquette.

BUSINESS CARDS

A business card is key to establishing yourself in the professional world. Hand them out to your friends, family, new and old acquaintances, and anyone else you think may help you. Also remember to ask for others' cards and save them; building a large file of business cards can pay off in the future. Keep in mind, however, that it is usually inappropriate for a junior person to ask a senior person for a card. Feel free to give your card in return, but make sure your superior initiates the process.

When you get a card, jot a few notes on the back—how you met the person, the issues you discussed, and any personal information that you have in common. Keep the cards in a centralized location like a daily planner or a special three-ring binder with plastic sheets designed to hold business cards. Contact the card owners at least once a year to keep the lines of communication open. Many people send a holiday card to everyone on their list; the marginal cost can help build your professional image and create a powerful personal network.

THANK-YOU NOTES

There will be times when you need to write a personal thank-you note to a colleague, client, or prospective client. When you receive a gift, secure a new client, or have a great business dinner, it is a good idea to thank the person. This can be done a few different ways, but the most effective is to make the note as personal as possible. Address your note by hand, including the return address, and use a stamp instead of a postage meter. Write the note on blank stationery or on a thank-you card instead of on your letterhead. Remember this is your personal thank-you note. Write a few simple sentences that thank the person, describe the gift (or dinner), and encourage further contact. This simple tool can help build your career and keep you on top of your etiquette.

October 22, 2001

Dear Mrs. Smith,

   Thank you for meeting with me today to discuss ABC company. I appreciate the time you took to explain the new job and its responsibilities. I hope that we get the chance to work together on the XYZ project!

Sincerely,
Clint

PLANE TRAVEL

The incidence of air travel, especially for business pur-
poses, is increasing at steady rates. Corporate meetings
and trade conferences in various parts of the country may
make flying a necessity. Although flying etiquette is
rather simple, it is certainly important enough to be covered here. Pack lightly and sensibly. Make sure to include
the essentials, but do not overburden yourself with too
many accessories or unnecessary items. You may want to
call your hotel to see if your room will be equipped with
a blow dryer, iron, and ironing board. If the hotel pro-
vides these important items, you can save yourself a lot of
packing space. Whenever possible, bring only one carry-
on suitcase and keep it small enough to fit below the seat
in front of you. In it, include reading material, a change
of underwear and attire, a razor, and a toothbrush. Delays
can happen when you least expect them and usually at
the most inopportune time. It's always better to prepare
yourself by carrying something you can change into—
just in case.

When you reach your seat, realize that most passen-
gers are interested in their reading or other matters.
They would probably prefer not to talk to you, even if
you are charming and entertaining. Bring some reading
material, usually more than you think you'll need. If
you're delayed, you'd much rather be reading something
of your choice than the latest SkyMall catalog.

Here are a few tips for the frequent flyer:

- Join all the frequent flyer programs you can. They're free and can quickly pay for themselves.
- Try to sit in exit rows. They have a little more legroom and are usually free of small children.
- Remember that alcohol affects you more at higher altitudes, so limit the number of cocktails you order.
- If you fly a particular airline often, consider joining one of the pay clubs that offers a more relaxed setting, office equipment, and some amenities that the average traveler doesn't get.

Dating in the Office

Dating in the office is usually frowned on, but in the real world, it often occurs. When you spend hours each day with someone, if there is some sort of romantic spark, it will often catch fire. So what do you do? The first step is to consider company policies. Most companies discourage romance between employees at different levels because of the perceived impropriety. Be sure that your company does not explicitly prohibit dating. After reviewing the risks and company polices, if you still decide to continue the relationship, do your best to keep the personal side separate from the business side. There is no excuse for spending time at work on your love life. Realize as well that if the relationship leads to something serious like marriage, the company might request that one or both of you transfer or even resign to avoid the appearance of impropriety.

RESIGNING FROM A JOB

If you're leaving your present employer, we hope it's because you've just taken a huge job offer from a great company. But no matter the reason, sometimes you have to resign from a position. Although some companies have stringent rules on how to terminate employment, most rules are not very strict. The best way to leave a company is to show respect for your employer's business and your coworkers. Basically, this means that you should give them a reasonable amount of time (at least two weeks) to find a replacement and to have you train that person before you go. Although you might have been treated poorly at this job, resist the urge to get back at your old employer. Do not take office supplies, ruin client relationships, or make the transition difficult. Word gets around in the business community; don't say or do anything that you wouldn't want your prospective employer to hear about. Unprofessional behavior is not tolerated (even if you think it's warranted). Besides, burning bridges is rarely a good business decision. You never know when your paths might cross again. Your best bet is to be happy (and perhaps relieved) that you'll be working at a new job soon.

CANCELING MEETINGS

Although canceling meetings is somewhat common, you should not do it lightly. A meeting, by definition, involves more than one person; so if you have to cancel, you'll be affecting at least one other person's schedule.

Before scrapping the meeting entirely, consider the chance that someone else can go in your stead or that the others can still meet and accomplish some of the planned objectives. If neither of these alternatives is appropriate, call the other person(s) as soon as you are certain that the meeting cannot take place and offer a suggestion that will work instead. It might be a teleconference, a live-chat, or even another meeting at another time; but put forth some alternatives before just canceling. Realize also that you have made other people's schedules more complicated, so be understanding and willing to compromise your schedule a bit for their convenience.

Using Sick Days and Vacation Days

We all get sick. We all need vacations. However, most employees don't know the best ways to use these days off. The first thing you should do is become familiar with your company's policy. Many companies group sick days and vacation days. This keeps illness-prone workers from using up too much company time and rewards healthy employees. Other companies have a set amount of time for both sick days and vacation days. Still more companies offer a "mental health" day each month. Be sure you know what kind of day you are taking before you call in to notify your boss.

If you are sick and you think that your illness is contagious, take the day off. Your coworkers do not want you to infect them, and your body could use the downtime.

Most illnesses can be cured in a day or two if you allow yourself enough rest. Be sure you know ahead of time the name of the person to call, his or her extension, and when to place the call. You will probably need to call at a reasonable morning hour, usually by eight or nine o'clock, in order to give everyone enough time to plan their day around your absence.

Most companies have set guidelines for when and how you can take vacation days. For example, most accounting firms are usually unwilling to allow vacations from the beginning of the year through April 15. Other companies require employees to give six weeks' notice before taking vacation days. So be sure to check before you make any plans that you wouldn't want to break. If no formal structures are in place, give a reasonable amount of notice—at least two weeks—so that company plans can be changed if need be. If you consider the needs of your employer when taking sick days and requesting vacation time, you will avoid creating problems and inconveniences—and you'll also keep your sanity!

MISCELLANEOUS TIPS

Here are a few other useful etiquette tips:

- If you have a kitchen or coffee station in your office, don't be afraid to make coffee. Be sure to clean up after yourself. Spend an extra three minutes to clean up a mess or wash a dish or two, and you will generate an amazing amount of goodwill.

- When walking with coworkers, be courteous. If you walk slowly or quickly, adjust your speed to accommodate the others in your group.

- If you feel a sneeze or cough coming on, use your left hand and a tissue to cover your nose and mouth. This leaves your right hand free, if need be, to shake hands.

- Part of keeping up your image is staying fiscally responsible. At one extreme, this means avoiding personal bankruptcy. At the other extreme, it means being conscious of your wealth and not allowing it to change you as a person. Money can be a wonderful tool in life, but it should not be your ultimate goal.

SHAKING HANDS 18

All it takes is three seconds, but the handshake is an important component in that very powerful first impression. The moment you are introduced to someone, or when the prospective employer is a few feet away from you, extend your right hand. You should find a happy medium here: a firm handshake is best. There was a time when deals were sealed with a handshake. Remember, you want the person you are meeting to know that you are a solid person who can be trusted and counted on. On the flip side, do not injure the person you are meeting. You want to make the person feel good.

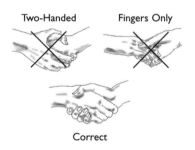

Two-Handed   Fingers Only

Correct

When the opportunity presents itself, square your shoulders to the person you want to greet. Smile, look them in the eye, and extend your right hand. Your fingers should be relatively close to each other, but not actually touching, and your thumb should be pointed straight up. As your hand meets the other hand, try to touch your thumb-finger web to that of the other person. Next, place your thumb on his or her hand, and squeeze it as if you were squeezing the ketchup out of a plastic container. Shake for about three pumps and then slowly pull your hand away.

If you are at an occasion that requires nametags, be sure to place the nametag on your right breast pocket to make it easier for others to read your name when you shake their hand. At a cocktail party, for example, keep your drink in your left hand. Since you will shake with your right hand, you do not want it to be cold and wet from the glass. If the other person's hand is wet, cold, or sweaty, don't draw attention to the condition, even in a joking manner. Act as if it were normal and move on. By politely ignoring it, you will help the other person feel more comfortable with you.

Some people, because of a disability, are unable to shake with their right hand. They are probably used to shaking with their left hand or in some other way. The best advice here is to watch them and follow their lead. If they offer to shake with their left hand and approach your left side, shake left hands. If they go for your right, they will cup their hand around the top of yours. Smile acceptingly and move on.

As odd as it sounds, practice shaking hands with family members or friends. Your goal is to let the other person know that you have a strong handshake without breaking any bones. A good handshake will help you present a strong first impression and illustrate your attention to detail.

Any discussion of professional conduct would be incomplete without a discussion of table manners. Many professional meetings begin, include, or conclude with a meal. Although good manners may not explicitly help you, bad manners will definitely hurt you.

The Table Setting

To get your bearings, look at the following illustration of a typical table setting. The simplest rule for using silverware is to work from the outside in toward the plate as the meal progresses. Your fork is on the left. If there are two forks, the smaller, outside one is the salad fork, and the larger, inner one is the dinner fork. On the right, from the outside, is your soupspoon and knife with its blade facing toward the plate. A spoon or fork found above your plate is for dessert. Your beverage and coffee cup will be located on the upper right corner of your table setting. Your salad plate will be on your left side with your bread plate.

EATING

As soon as you sit down at the table with others, find your napkin, unfold it, and put it on your lap. When ordering, be sure to think about how easy the food will be to eat. Maybe pasta is not the best choice for your meal. You should also think about what your associates will be eating and try to match your meal to theirs. For example, if they have a four-course dinner in mind, you might want to think again about getting just soup and a salad.

When you begin to eat, leave your nondominant hand on your lap or on the edge of the table and keep it there for most of the meal. You will want to eat with your dominant hand. The only time you will use both hands is to cut your food. To cut properly, hold your fork upside down with your nondominant hand and your knife with your dominant hand. As soon as you have finished cutting, place the knife back on the right side of the plate or across the top of the plate, and switch your fork to your dominant hand to eat.

When eating bread, break off a small piece, butter it, and eat it. Do not butter the whole piece of bread or roll all at once. Also do not cut your food into many pieces. Simply cut off the piece you will eat, chew it well, and then cut again. Use your napkin often to clean any crumbs or food pieces from your lips. When someone asks you to pass the salt or pepper, pass both at the same time. Never reach across anyone's "personal space." Ask the person to pass the item to you or pass it to him or her to pass farther down the table.

It may seem obvious, but don't talk with food in your mouth. If you are asked a question and your mouth is full, wait to finish chewing before you answer. Nothing is more embarrassing than beginning to talk and watching part of your meal fly across the table. In a professional setting, you should also focus on taking smaller bites. This will help you avoid a long pause while you chew your food after being asked a question.

If you get up during the meal, place your napkin on your chair. This lets the wait staff know that you will be returning soon. When you finish with a spoon, place it on the saucer under your soup dish or coffee cup, not in the bowl.

As soon as you have finished your meal, place your knife across the top of the plate, with the blade facing you. Next place your fork and other used utensils closer to the middle of the plate, tines down and parallel to the knife. Use your napkin to wipe your mouth, fold it loosely, and place it on the table. If you follow these simple rules, you will greatly lessen the chances of committing a serious faux pas at a business meal.

Paying for the Meal

Paying for meals is often a confusing element of etiquette, but there are generally accepted rules you can follow. The most basic rule is that the person who issues the invitation usually pays for the meal.

Next, if a question arises over payment, take the bill and treat your companions to a nice meal. Paying most of the time gives you several advantages over your tablemates. First, there is an inherent tendency to be somewhat indebted to the person who buys your meal. Second, you eliminate the awkwardness of waiting for someone else to pick up the tab.

Most businesses will expect their employees to pay when they entertain clients. If the client does take the bill, be sure to get it the next time and at least alternate paying. Avoid letting your clients pay for too many of your meals.

You will probably not be eating with your superiors on a regular basis, so it is acceptable for them to pay for the meal. But, if you usually eat with them, expect to pay for yourself most of the time. One caveat: If you invite your superior out to eat for a special purpose—for example, to ask for a raise or a promotion—you should pay.

The same thought process applies to eating with your subordinates. You probably won't do it very often. Make it a point to pay for their meals some of the time, but avoid paying every time. They may begin to expect it. When eating with your peers, you should usually pay your own way, but it's nice to pick up the check every once in a while.

Building Relationships

If you are in sales, or if you usually take your clients out to lunch or dinner, following these tips can help you and your career. When you invite someone to eat, you are making a big impression. Unfortunately, just issuing the invitation does not necessarily mean that the impression will be a good one.

The best way to prepare yourself to make good impressions is to build relationships with local restaurants near your office and around town. Pick three or four that serve a variety of foods, and one or two with a special theme or menu. You should visit these places at least once a month. Tip very well—at least 25 to 30 percent—and be friendly with the host or hostess and servers. After a few visits, ask them to give you an account. They can either bill you at the end of each month or keep your credit card on file and charge all your meals to it. Either way, make sure that many of the servers and the host or hostess knows who you are and treats you with respect.

These relationships allow you to focus on the business at hand, knowing that you will have great service and that the bill will not be an issue. In addition, you will be able to get a great table on short notice, you will not have to wait to be seated, and you will get excellent service.

Once you have your relationships firmly in place, you will have more flexibility when making plans with your clients. Ask them where they will be before you plan to eat, and cater the invitation to that location. This will also give you a bit of an edge because you will be in a comfortable and familiar environment. You will avoid many of the hassles that spring up when eating out, and your clients will be impressed by your good rapport with the staff and your excellent attention to detail.

STAYING ORGANIZED

Staying organized is a huge part of being successful in business. Although a clean and organized desk will not guarantee a promotion, it will definitely help you find and process material quickly. Work to keep your office or cubicle clean; clients and superiors will be put off by a messy workplace. Consider instituting a good filing system using hanging folders or other organizational tools. Don't be afraid to rid your desk of papers that will not serve you in the future. Your trashcan should be your most used filing device.

Planning is the key to good time organization, so get a good daily planner or handheld device. Many different styles are available; as long as you use the planner, the type doesn't matter. First, make sure that it allows you to plan on a daily, weekly, monthly, and long-term basis. It should also have room for names, addresses, and phone numbers. Some planners even have clear plastic sheets that can hold about six business cards per page. Keep the cards you use most in these pages. For the others that you accumulate, use a three-ring binder with 10-card sheets to keep them in an accessible, portable form.

Many professionals supplement their planners by including a "to-do" list with the major items for the day, in order of importance. You can either do this in your planner or print out a sheet on your computer and replace it as you see fit. You might also choose to keep your key names and addresses in the planner on sheets from your computer. The idea is to include as much helpful and useful information in your planner as possible. When you need to contact someone, it is a wonderful feeling to know, beyond a shadow of a doubt, that you have his or her information in your planner.

BEING ON TIME

Not everyone finds it easy to be on time. Most people who arrive on time and call when they say they will have to work at it. Professionals must become masters of time. Making a point of being on time is an obvious way of showing your attention to detail. People who are known for punctuality are also well respected and trusted.

When arriving for a meeting, show up about one to five minutes before the scheduled time. You do not want to rush someone by showing up too much before your set time. On the other hand, being late shows a lack of consideration. If you become unavoidably detained, call. Use your mobile phone or a pay phone, but be sure to make the call. Realize, however, that you should make every effort to be on time. The first time you meet someone at an unfamiliar location—or if you are concerned about being late—plan on arriving fifteen to twenty minutes early. You can use this extra time in your car or outside the building to deal with small administrative tasks such as catching up on phone calls, organizing your briefcase, reading a report, planning a meeting, or dictating a memo.

OFFICE POLITICS 21

"People will talk." You have heard it before, but at work, it is much more prevalent. When you finally get your job, you will find office politics and the proverbial "grapevine" not only exist but also often run rampant. You must be prepared for this; expect it and accept it.

This does not mean that you have to play the game. It is very easy to sit with your coworkers and complain about your boss, other coworkers, or subordinates, but it is not in good taste. Simply put: Do not do it. There is no good reason to sit in on these discussions, let alone participate in them. The information—or misinformation—is harmful not only to the subjects of the discussion but to the speaker and the listener as well. By participating, you often gather faulty information. Also, if you tell others how you dislike someone with whom you are usually pleasant, they will realize that they cannot trust your motives or anything you say. Rise above gossip. Stick to your work and the tasks that will help you succeed. You will be stronger and more respected for it in the end.

When you work to develop a friendly rapport with your coworkers, be smart about it. A proven plan is to be respectful with everyone and give possible friendships plenty of time to develop. People respond well when they are treated with respect. Most office friendships are best developed slowly. If you make your coworkers feel comfortable by treating them with respect, you will build strong relationships over time.

When first building these relationships, be wary of constantly going out after work with your new coworkers. A drink or two after work can be a very good idea, but keep it to one or two. The key to after-hours socialization is to limit its time and extent; learn the fine art of leaving people wanting more. Becoming too friendly too soon often results in an awkward relationship that may turn ugly. There are several benefits to getting to know your fellow workers outside the office. Just remember to give the relationships time to develop. Along the same vein, be extremely careful when dating someone from the office. These romances usually end badly and can destroy careers.

When you're in the office, or even in an after-hours social setting, act as if every action you take is being recorded. This is a cynical view, but it is the safest course to follow. Refrain from making lewd jokes because they will almost certainly offend someone. Similarly, do not imitate someone who stutters or has an accent. This type of mocking behavior is cruel and rude. It almost always gets back to the person you are imitating and definitely harms you. Even if you think you are funny, you are still out of line. Remember, if you treat people with respect, you will build strong relationships with your coworkers.

The exponential increase in sexual harassment cases proves that any touching, of either men or women, is inappropriate in the professional environment. Although it is somewhat awkward, you must avoid physical contact

with your coworkers in the professional setting. It illustrates your respect for their "personal space," as well as
your professionalism. By treating your coworkers with
respect, you will immediately show your exemplary professional conduct.

22 STAYING INFORMED

There is an obvious need to stay informed about current events that affect your company, profession, and industry. If your biggest competitor files for bankruptcy, it is important for you to have a basic knowledge about what happened and what the impact might be on you and your company.

There are many things you can learn about the world by keeping up to date. People are often judged by their ability to engage in small talk. It is imperative to be able to speak intelligently with your coworkers. The Internet is full of sites that provide quick and clear news to help you stay informed. Look at *www.cnn.com*, *www.yahoo.com*, and *www.cnbc.com*.

Most professionals need to have at least a rudimentary knowledge of the issues facing the world today. The reason is that in many of the "relaxed professional settings" when small talk is prevalent, the discussion often turns to current events. It is quite embarrassing when your boss questions you about your thoughts on a new political issue and you have no idea what it is, let alone what you think about it.

Remember that current events will come up in daily conversation, and it pays to know something about them. You are constantly being judged; by keeping up to date, you can really show off your attention to detail.

Golf Etiquette 23

A great deal of business is conducted on the golf course and knowing the proper etiquette can help you seal the deal. At the same time, you can quickly make a fool out of yourself if you stumble over the rules, both written and unwritten. Although a complete guide on golf etiquette could take volumes, this chapter should give you some of the basics.

First, you need to understand why golf and business are so closely tied. It is a simple fact that in about four hours on a golf course you can learn a great deal about those with whom you play. Integrity, skill under pressure, class, personal habits, risk-tolerance levels, and etiquette are all exposed. Golf is a surrogate for spending years getting to know someone. In this somewhat competitive arena, shrouded with class and dignity, a person's true nature is exposed. Think of it as a minibattle; your true mettle is tested and you either win or lose.

Ambiguity in golf is not an option. Almost every professional should have a general understanding of the game of golf and its rules. It is also advisable to take a few lessons so you'll have a basic level of competence if you are invited to play. Although it may not be your game of choice, it is often chosen in the business world.

You will limit your chances for improvement, promotions, and new business by not knowing the basics.

GOLF TERMS

Golf terminology is unlike that used in other sports—it does not make a whole lot of sense. Scoring is based on the total number of *strokes* (times you hit the ball) you take in the *round* (18 holes of play); the lower the better. *Par* is the number of strokes it should take you to hit the ball from the *tee box* (where you start) to the *fairway* (the middle section), the *green*, and into the hole. There are three basic kinds of holes: Par 3s, 4s, and 5s. The higher the par number is, the longer the hole is in yards. If you *shoot* (score) par on a hole, you've done well. One over par is a *bogey*, two over is a *double bogey*, and so on. If you are one under par, you've made a *birdie*. If, somehow, you make two under par, you've got an *eagle* and have done a wonderful job. (You might want to consider retiring and trying out for the PGA tour if this becomes a regular occurrence.)

You might also hear, or have to yell, "Fore!" This is a standard golf warning meaning that a ball is coming at you at a high rate of speed. The standard response is to hit the deck and cover your head. Although you might look a bit silly diving down, not heeding this warning can be quite painful.

DRESSING AND ACTING THE PART

Dressing for golf is a huge part of the game. The late Payne Stewart was one of the only modern professional golfers to wear old-style knickers. Although dressing in these early styles is not necessary, dressing properly for modern golf is mandatory. This means a collared shirt and usually slacks (not jeans); although in some hot-weather climates, shorts are acceptable. If you are unsure, call the club or your host to see if shorts can be worn. You should bring golf shoes with you, but wear your street shoes to the club and change in the locker room, not in the parking lot.

Keep just a few items in your pockets: two extra balls, some tees, a divot repair tool, and a ball marker. You can use a dime as a marker, but be sure it does not make noise in your pocket. You should also keep some cash on you; gambling is not mandatory on the course, but it is often present and you must be prepared in case you lose.

Cell phones are quickly becoming the scourge of the golf course as more and more golfers spend quite a lot of time during the rounds on the phone. Although it is commendable that these golfers want to be reachable and work, the golf course is not the place. If you have an important deal that is constantly interrupting the game, you should not be playing. Many private courses are "Cell Phone Free Zones," and some are even installing blocking devices that will jam any signal around the course. Although you will probably not be asked to leave if your phone rings, it is considered extremely poor etiquette to place or receive calls during the round.

If you need the security of your phone, turn it off or make it silent and keep it in your bag. If you then find the need to use your phone, be sure to clear it with your host or those with whom you are playing before you start talking. Keep it short and between holes, but if at all possible, save it for the clubhouse after the round. At worst, wait until you reach the halfway house where you can get a drink or snack. As the name implies, it splits the *front* (first) nine holes and the *back* (last) nine holes.

Rules

When playing, there are a few rules to keep in mind. First and foremost, *do not cheat*. This may seem obvious but it bears repeating. Remember, businesspeople use golf as a surrogate for actually getting to know you, so any breach of honesty or integrity will be magnified. Count your score honestly because others will. They might not yell out "Liar! You had a seven not a five!" but they will not forget that you shaved your score. This also applies to your *lie;* that is, where the ball sits on the course. Often, players will nudge it onto a nice patch of grass, away from a stone or branch. Someone almost always sees this, and it is against the rules.

There are two exceptions to this rule. One occurs when your ball lands in a "ground-under-repair" area, usually marked by a white circle. The other exception is if you are playing under winter rules, a northern phenomenon used in early spring and late fall. Although not officially recognized by the PGA, winter rules basically state that if the ball lies in a weather damaged area like a huge puddle, you can move it out of the area, but no closer to the hole, without a penalty.

You will sometimes hear other players suggest that you "take a better lie" or "hit that one over." Do not accept these offers. Simply smile and say, "Thanks, but I think I can play that." Although it might add a few strokes to your game, it will earn you some great etiquette points.

Do not be afraid to ask questions when you are confused. If the rules or betting seem beyond your scope of understanding (and many bets are extremely complicated), ask for clarification. It is much harder to get clarification after you have broken a rule or lost a bet, and more damaging to the ego. This also applies to the course itself. If you are unsure of the layout of the hole, ask someone who has played there before. You might say something like "If I'm somehow able to hit the ball properly, where should I aim?" Self-effacing humor, remember, is a great way to get others to help you.

Other rules of golf etiquette are common sense. For example, do not talk or make noise while someone is swinging or putting. You might ruin their concentration and lose a friend. If you make a divot during your swing, replace it and pat it down. Some courses will give you a green sand mixture that has grass seed in it to pour on top of the divot as well. When on the green, repair ball marks that you or others have left. There is nothing worse than a putt going offline because someone did not take care of the green.

When someone is hitting, there are two acceptable places to stand: directly behind the person so he or she cannot see you or at least seven feet in front of the person, facing his or her right shoulder. Never stand directly behind (or for that matter in front of) the line of flight of the ball. You will either distract the other person or get hit; neither option is very appealing.

If you have the misfortune of hitting your ball into a sand trap, remember to rake it clean after you hit the ball out. If one of your fellow golfers is stuck in a sand trap, it is considered good etiquette to hand him or her a rake after the shot so that it is easier to rake the trap.

A quick golf rule: *If you are in the trap, also called a hazard, you may not let your club hit the sand until you swing at the ball. A real stickler for the rules might just catch you off guard, so be careful!*

Although there are hundreds of other rules that are considered "good etiquette," these will help you get a good start. The benefits that come from a well played round of golf are more than worth the time it takes to learn the basics. If you can become a good "corporate golfer" who follows the rules and etiquette, you will reap the rewards tenfold.

DATING ETIQUETTE

Dating is one of the most confusing rituals in our society. However, if you follow the simple rules outlined here, and have a little luck, it can also be one of the most enjoyable. The process of dating can be incredibly complex, but if you stick to the most important rule—honesty—the rest of the ritual can be managed. The importance of the first date cannot be overstated. In a few hours, you get the chance to make a first impression, learn some key points about your date, show respect, and set the tone for the entire relationship. Remember, on this date especially, that your etiquette can make or break your chances. If you follow the rules of dating and basic etiquette, you can quickly show your date that you have a basic level of respect for her, which is quite beneficial to your dating future.

GOALS

Before starting any venture, it is a good idea to know what your goals might be. Dating is no different. What are you looking for? Is this your quest to find "the one" or are you just looking for a fun relationship? Be sure to decide what you want before the date—and be sure your date knows your intentions as well. It is unfair to both of you if either one is looking for different things in a relationship, so know what you want and be honest about your intentions.

THE DATE

Dressing for a date is not nearly as simple as dressing for work. However, you do have a bit more flexibility. No specific look is better or worse than another, the key is to wear appropriate clothing for your activities. If you are going to a picnic, do not wear a suit; if you are off to the opera, jeans will not work. It is important to stick with your style and wear something that makes you feel comfortable. The key to your appearance is to take attention away from the clothes and put it on to the date. Remember that people judge you by the way you look, so be sure to look good, whatever you wear.

Dating behavior, while similar to the other rules of etiquette, is a bit more specific. First, turn your cell phone off. You will not look cool or important by having your phone ring all night long—you will look insensitive, though. If you see some of your friends while you are out on the date, introduce them and make everyone feel comfortable. It is also important to tip well. It shows your date that you are considerate and appreciative.

Be sure to tip the valet, the cab driver, the coatroom attendant, the waiter or waitress, and the bartender.

For some reason, eating and dating are tied together. This odd coupling makes any date harder because the rules and chances for either of you to make a mistake increase incredibly. Be careful about what you order; if the food is messy, you can make a fool out of yourself rather quickly. Eat with your mouth closed, wipe your mouth if you might have food on or around it, and be sure you don't have food stuck in your teeth. When paying for a meal, don't make it the focus of the evening. Especially on the first date, it's a good idea to have your credit card ready so you can pull out your card and pay as soon as you see the check. Although the woman might offer to pay, simply say "Thank you, but I would like to get this one," and end the conversation. If she insists, do not take the opportunity to start an argument. Be sure not to dwell on it—you did not go on the date to see who would pay for the meal.

Conversation is the lifeblood of the date, so focus some of your energy on making it work. For starters, you can avoid the touchy subjects of sex, religion, politics, and past relationships. Again, be honest and sincere; these are two keys to beginning a successful relationship. Be sure to make eye contact, be yourself, and engage the person in a two-way conversation. The easiest way to do this is to ask open-ended questions instead of questions that elicit simple yes or no answers.

AFTER THE DATE

After the date, you will usually find yourself in a precarious spot. Either you really want to see her again, or you really do not. If you are not interested, do not say you'll call. Leading someone on is unacceptable and will eventually come back to haunt you. You do not have to explain that you never want to see her again; make it clear that you enjoyed her company and wish her the best.

If you are interested in this woman and want to see her again, the question of when to call becomes an issue. If you really like her and you think she had a great time too, you might to call the next day. It is standard to wait a day or two after the date before you call, and you will rarely go wrong with this time frame. The problem with calling too soon is that you seem too eager; if you wait too long, your date may lose interest. The secret is there is no real secret, no steadfast rule. Go with your gut instinct—if you're right, great. If you're wrong, learn from it and you will be that much smarter the next time around. There is no magic bullet in dating; but if you follow the basic rules, with a little luck, you will be able find the right relationship for you.

CALLER-ID

One of the new tools of technology that has revolution-ized dating is Caller-ID. It can be a great tool for you, and a huge problem as well. First, assume that everyone you date has Caller-ID and knows every time you call. This will limit the number of times you call and alter the meaning of the times you do not get an answer. You must limit the number of times you call, especially if you don't leave a message. There is nothing worse for your dating future than having your date see that she had twenty-five new calls, all of which came from you. It is also important to realize that your date may be home and is just not interested in answering your call. Don't just assume that since you called and didn't reach her you don't have to leave a message. Calling and not leaving a message is rude. So after you've called and haven't heard back, wait a day or two before calling back. If you still haven't heard back, this relationship probably isn't going to proceed any further.

CONCLUSION

With the simple techniques discussed in this book, you can begin to take command of your professional demeanor. People will notice your attention to detail and realize that you care about your professional reputation. If you keep your appearance in order and act like a gentleman, you will probably find that you are treated with respect. But most important, you will feel more comfortable about yourself and be able to do your best work. Remember, attention to detail can be a great help to your career and to your life.

If you have any thoughts, ideas, suggestions, questions, or comments, please send them to:

Attention to Detail Newsletter
Greenleaf Book Group LLC,
660 Elmwood Point
Aurora, Ohio 44202
You can also call us at (800) 932-5420
Visit our Web site at *www.greenleafenterprises.com*
E-mail us at *atd@greenleafenterprises.com*.

ABOUT THE AUTHOR

Clint Greenleaf is chairman and CEO of Greenleaf Enterprises, Inc. and Greenleaf Book Group LLC. He spent three years training in the United States Marine Corps ROTC program before graduating with a B.A. in economics/accounting from The College of the Holy Cross in Worcester, Massachusetts. While in college, he worked as an admissions officer interviewing high school seniors for entry into Holy Cross; this is when he noticed a need for such a book. After graduation, he worked at Deloitte & Touche, a "Big 5" accounting firm and passed the CPA exam.

GREENLEAF ENTERPRISES

For more information on professional appearance and etiquette, visit *www.greenleafenterprises.com* or call (800) 932-5420.

SELECTED BIBLIOGRAPHY

The Amy Vanderbilt Complete Book of Etiquette. Nancy Tuckerman and Nancy Dunnan. Doubleday: New York, NY, 1995.

Attention to Detail: A Gentleman's Guide to Professional Appearance and Conduct. Clinton T. Greenleaf III. Greenleaf Enterprises, Inc.: Cleveland, OH, 1998.

Beyond Hello. Jeannie Davis. Now Hear This Publishing: Denver, CO, 1999.

The Business Card Book. Lynella Grant. Off the Page Press: Tuscon, AZ, 1998.

Business Etiquette: 101 Ways to Conduct Business with Charm and Savvy. Ann Marie Sabath. Career Press, 1998.

Complete Guide to Executive Manners. Letitia Baldridge. Rawson Associates, 1985.

The Elements of Style. Strunk and White. Allyn and Bacon, 2000.

Emily Post's Etiquette. Peggy Post. HarperCollins: New York, NY, 1997.

Everyday Business Etiquette. Marilyn Pincus. Barrons: New York, NY, 1996.

Executive Etiquette. Marjabelle Young Stewart. St. Martin's Griffin: New York, NY, 1996.

A Gentleman's Guide to Appearance. Clinton T. Greenleaf III. Adams Media Corporation: Avon, MA, 2000.

The Gentleman's Guide to Life. Steve Friedman. Three Rivers Press: New York, NY, 1997.

Golf Etiquette 101. Bill Bailey. Prima: Roseville, CA, 1998.

How to Be a Gentleman. John Bridges. Rutledge Hill Press: Nashville, TN, 1998.

Men's Wardrobe (Chic Simple). Kim Johnson Gross. Knopf: New York, NY, 1998.

Wireless Etiquette. Peter Laufer. Omnipoint Corporation: Boston, MA, 1999.

INDEX

eating, 73-75. *See also table
manners*
Elements of Style, The
(Strunk and White),
32
elevator etiquette, 58
eye contact, 25

F
face-to-face
communication, 25
fiscal responsibility, 68
formal wear, 4
foul language, 28-29

G
golf etiquette, 85-90

H
handshakes, 69-71
humor, 15

I
Internet use, 38-39
interviews
questions during,
50-51, 53
dining during, 52
discussions at, 49-50
follow-up after, 53-54
preparation for, 48-49

L
language, 28-29
letters
business, 32-34
thank-you, 53-54, 62
loyalty, 14

M
meetings, canceling,
65-66

N
nonverbal
communication, 23-24
notes, taking, 25

O
office accessories, 7
office politics, 81-83
office romance, 64
organization, 78-79

P
personal accessories, 7-8
personal calls, 26-27
personal interactions
with clients, 20
consideration in, 14-15
humor in, 15
loyalty in, 14
platinum rule in, 16-17
responsibility in, 13-14